Haikus for Cats

Jacob Levin

Haikus for Cats
Copyright © 2023 by Jacob Levin

All rights reserved. No part of this publication may be reproduced, distributed, or transmitted in any form or by any means, including photocopying, recording, or other electronic or mechanical methods, without the prior written permission of the publisher, except in the case of brief quotations embodied in critical reviews and certain other noncommercial uses permitted by copyright law.

ISBN-13: 979-8-3924-284-0-3

Interior Formatting by Streetlight Graphics

Introduction

Haikus for… Cats? "But wait!" (I hear you say.) "Cat's can't read!" Or can they?

No, cats can't read, but they do like chewing a good book. Meanwhile, based on my experience, most cat owners can read. And they do. A lot.

So what better way for a cat owner to appreciate their cat more than to read some brief, witty, cat haikus? I can't think of any, can you?

So read on, Cat Person.

Welcome to "Haikus for Cats," a collection of 121 witty and insightful poems that capture the essence of our feline friends. These haikus are inspired by the daily quirks and habits of cats, from their insatiable curiosity to their graceful movements and occasional mischievousness.

Each poem is a brief but evocative snapshot of the world through a cat's eyes, inviting the reader to contemplate the mysteries and pleasures of life as seen from a feline perspective. Whether you're a dedicated cat lover or simply appreciate the art of poetry, "Haikus for Cats" offers a delightful and charming glimpse into the world of our feline companions.

Jacob Levin, Esq.

I dedicate this book and all the laughs to my grandmother, Helen Stern, who loved cats and made all of her kids and grandkids pretty crazy about cats, too. Also, to my childhood cats, Tango and Peter, and to my current cats, Yenta and Tevya (Fiddler on the Roof, much?), and to my future cats, should I merit to love more cats in this lifetime.

Haikus for Cats

Jacob Levin

I grapple, I fight!

With all my heart and nine lives

An untied shoelace

A vegan diet?

What am I supposed to do?

There's nothing to kill

Y ou might not pick up

On our subtle signs of love

Purring decibels

Alliteration

We cats sure can turn a phrase

Turkey and tuna

You just keep swimming

Just pretend like I'm not here

My owner's goldfish

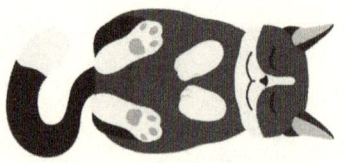

I used to fit in

your shoe; now I'm way too big

Pains of growing old

*E*arly bird gets worm

That's okay with me because

Early cat gets bird

*S*tuck up in this tree

Stupid bird staring at me

It was well worth it

Stuck in a shelter

Awaiting that special one

To call mine for good

Knocked off all the plants

Puked all over the floor — I'm

Just getting started

Sleep most of the day

Never respond to my name

Cat philosophy

All ferocious cat

This king takes up half the floor

Then the doorbell rings

Here, this is your gift

I killed it because I think

You're a bad hunter

Sharp fangs protruding

The all-courageous hunter

Drinks from the faucet

Stealthy, skilled huntress

Stalks calmly across the plains

Headfirst in food bag

Brave neighborhood guard

Proud protector — fierce lion

Sleeps under my bed

Cat sitter does not

know my secret petting spots

Right between my ears

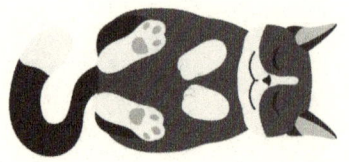

My warm fur, sunlight

Stretch, roll over, cute, you laugh

Never mind the barf

Damn fish swims; I watch

I will get you just wait! Splash!

I meant to do that

You call me "kitten"

    Even if the food bag says

                      I beg to differ

I might write a book

Contribute to the zeitgeist

"The art of the nap"

Knocked over a glass

Blamed the dog, got away clean

Cat's rule of the game

Watching the world go

From atop the bookshelf high

Such a grand tableau

Stretching in the sun

Whiskers twitching with delight

Life's simple pleasures

*L*apping up water

As if it's from the Nile's banks

Such royal poise

With a flick of tail

Slinking off to parts unknown

Mystery and charm

Knock things off table

Straight into my human's soul

Cat's ultimate goal

A curious soul

Poking nose into places

Where no one else goes

Boy I've got problems

No food, wet or dry — nothing

Can't be solved with sleep

Language humans speak

lots of sounds; I prefer one

Elegant meow

These are my kittens

I will bathe them with my tongue

Instincts tell me to

Pounce into that box?

Might be just a bit too snug

If I fit I fit

I lay peacefully

Yikes! Jump! What the hell was that??

Stupid cucumber

Cats can talk, you know

We tell it the way it is

Thus we stay quiet

What's this silly thing?

I'll push it off the counter

You can clean it up

Trying to join you

For dinner; your food smells good

Don't mind little me!

Schrödinger's theory

cat is both alive and dead

Is food wet and dry?

Paw prints on the floor

Cat hair next to broken glass

That's circumstantial

It's freezing outside

Poor dog has to pee out there

I've got cat litter

What is going on?

It's already 9 am!

Still, an empty bowl?

Inviting window

Three floors down and I'm O.K.

I still have eight lives

My paws make no sound

Only the sound of your vase

Shattered on the ground

Please shop Amazon

They have high quality things

Like those huge boxes

Slip on the tile floors

Poop in a cat litter box

The modern wild cat

Caugh aarg gu-blah-ka

That's just the noise of our sport

We call it "hairball"

Your expensive couch

Now full of my claws' design

I think it looks good

Raining cats and dogs?

That does not even make sense

We'd never hang out!

Pretend you're not here

I don't respond to my name

Just my cattitude

Always get my way

have someone change my litter

Cat Rules: 101

All I have I've earned:

Toys, organic food and love

I'm the mousekeeper

Stand perfectly still

wiggle butt — jump! I've trained at

The Acatemy

I lie on the bed

Watch you leave for work each day

Don't worry; I'll nap

Behind broken blinds

I gaze quietly at you

You don't know I'm here

When you are a cat

Everywhere is a cushion!

Complain and get bit

Let me in, meow!

Can't you hear me scratch the door?

Now please let me out

Coughed up a fur ball,

I'll wonder where that come from

While I lick myself

My owner's dinner

looks good — still missing something

A dash of cat hair

I'm a cat-lady

    meaning I'm a female cat

        What else could I mean?

I'm going to nap

Let me find the perfect spot

My owner's laptop

I fit in so smug

It's fun being a kitten

Get your own slipper

What's in that big bag?

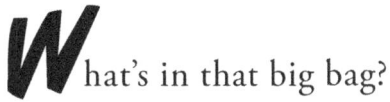

Smells like something edible

Nope; it's just darkness

If I get stressed out

I don't need therapy — I

Find myself a box

Don't you freaking dare!

What you doing? I'm a *cat*!

I don't do leashes

My head rubs you – *purr*

Eyes are large — my middle name

Insincerity

Slept most of the day

Groomed myself — had some catnip

It's called cat self-care

I sure love wheatgrass

It helps with my digestion

Then I throw it up

My owner's stomach;

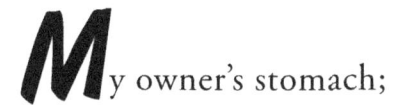

Fluffy like a batch of dough

Perfect for kneading

Stupid fireman

Pulled me out of the tree — I

Rule all I survey

Eww! Is that water?

I would never drink that stuff

I prefer gravy

Scratch my belly please

Not like that — what's wrong with you?

I can't talk; I bite

Keep a food supply

Wet, dry, water fountains too

Conditional love

Evolution-wise

Loud noises are predators

Now can openers

Meow meow me!

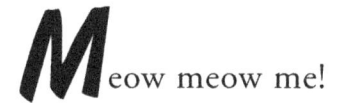

Did I say it's all about

Meow meow me?

I bite my owner

She looks at me all betrayed

We bite those we love

Whiskers on each side

Tells us if we can get through

And then retreat out

Cat hair everywhere

If you had one penny each

You could hire a maid

I'd like some tuna

Hey lady, open one now!

What are your thumbs for?

I am ferocious

I kill mice, birds and snakes too

Just let me outside

I sure love to hunt

Haven't you seen my sharp claws?

I was born with them

My guy's a lawyer

He buys me the best cat food

His briefcase smells nice

My tail wags and wags

Not the best time to pet me

Can't you take a hint?

Our vacuum cleaner

Broke vacuuming all my fur

Guess that means I won

Personalities

Cats are totally unique

But we all love fish

I sure hate my vet

pokes me with lots of needles

Owner just lets her

Hey cat! Hey cat! Hey!

Don't yell, we can hear you! We

Just don't give a shit

Why stop petting me?

Cats must be pet — it's in the

Cat Constitution

Change my litter please

Peed there *once* but don't forget

You adopted me

It's been *seven* years

That thing has been haunting me

The evil red dot

There are cat apps now!

I'd like an iPhone — just know

I won't text you back

Bet you didn't know

The truth is we love those mice

Killing them, that is

Refrigerator

A good place to hide behind

Don't be seen — just watch

On my rocking chair

Smells just like my owner's butt

I kinda like it

I love my owner

He barbecues all the time

And throws me the scraps

Sniffing the laundry

Rolling around in the clothes

I just love my life

Owner says I'm the

cutest cat he's ever owned

You can't "own" a cat

I love my hairbrush

Grooms me and pulls out loose fur

Make yourself a scarf

My human's bathing

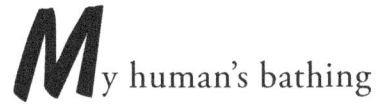

What a huge waste of water

You can use your tongue

So I hissed at you

Doesn't mean I'm not hungry

Feed me and then leave

King of the Jungle

That's how I feel when I'm on

Top of my cat tree

One leg stands up tall

Would you look the other way

While I take my bath?

Here's my gift to you

A mouse, dead; caught it myself

Goes with the others

My butt's on the rise

Thanks for scratching near my tail

It's hard to explain

Looking at that guy

ignoring me in my home

He's the lap I want

My bed is not yours

But *your* couch is mine and where

I sharpen my claws

I love killing mice

Hunt it, catch it, bring it home

Show it to my boss

My owner's a vet

A lot of cats are not fans

I kinda love her

Today's my birthday

    Human gives me special treat

        Human grade tuna

'm feeling relaxed

Everything is just so cool

Thanks for the catnip

Move at your own risk

I am content on your lap

Can't you feel me purr?

Cat food. Wet or dry?

generations of us ask

The old cat debate

Can I get a toy?

We love mice even fake ones

It's part of our charm

I see your couch is

scratched up. Don't judge I was just

A little kitten

Please oh please oh please

Don't declaw us — not humane

Souls are in our claws

You say I'm a cat

You might call it semantics;

I'm a small lion

Cats bring you good luck

But you already knew that

Why'd you think I'm here?

When I play with yarn

You think I'm adorable

I think it's a snake

It's not arrogance

I'm just a natural queen

I'm a calico

Is that a cat treat?

It's a trick! Damn door slams loud

Going to the vet

What are you cooking?

Smells like some kind of poultry

I'm not that picky

Sure my fur is soft

It's from the constant bathing

My personal spa

*T*o kill all the mice

Or to not kill all the mice

That's not a question

Made in the USA
Las Vegas, NV
16 December 2023